Seven Great Opera Overtures

in Full Score

Wolfgang Amadeus Mozart

DOVER PUBLICATIONS, INC.
Mineola, New York

Mozart's operas are available in the following Dover full-score editions:

0-486-27108-0 / **Idomeneo** [Breitkopf & Härtel ed.]

0-486-26004-6 / **Abduction from the Seraglio** [Breitkopf & Härtel ed.]

0-486-23751-6 / **The Marriage of Figaro** [C. F. Peters ed.]

0-486-23026-0 / **Don Giovanni** [C. F. Peters ed.]

0-486-24528-4 / **Così Fan Tutte** [authoritative ed., Ital. & Fr. texts]

0-486-24783-X / **The Magic Flute** [C. F. Peters ed.]

0-486-27540-X / **La Clemenza di Tito** [Breitkopf & Härtel ed.]

Bibliographical Note

This Dover edition, first published in 1998, is a new compilation of works originally published by Breitkopf & Härtel, Leipzig, n.d. [1881–2] as part of Serie 5: "Opern—Partitur—Overturen" in *Wolfgang Amadeus Mozart's Werke, Kritisch durchgesehene Gesammtausgabe.*
The Dover edition adds background information, an instrumentation list, and a new main heading for each work. The original German footnotes on pp. 40 and 82 have been replaced by an expanded editorial note on Contents p. iii.

International Standard Book Number: 0-486-40174-X

Manufactured in the United States of America
Dover Publications, Inc., 31 East 2nd Street, Mineola, N.Y. 11501

CONTENTS

OVERTURES TO THE OPERAS

NOTE: The endings of the overtures to *Die Entführung aus dem Serail* (see page 40) and *Don Giovanni* (see p. 82) were composed by the legendary music publisher Johann André for concert performances; the original endings lead directly into the opera. André, even more than Mozart scholars Otto Jahn and Ludwig von Köchel, is generally regarded as 'the father of Mozart research'. "It was Mozart's estate [purchased from the composer's widow, Constanze, in 1799] that gave André his life's task . . . producing from 1800 a veritable plentitude of . . . reliable 'editions following the composer's manuscript.'" (*Grove*, 1980: Vol. 1)

Idomeneo

Idomeneo, rè di Creta / Idomeneus, King of Crete

Opera seria in three acts

K366 (1781)

Libretto by Giambattista Varesco
based on the libretto *Idoménée* by Antoine Danchet (1712)

First performance: Residenztheater, Munich
29 January 1781

INSTRUMENTATION

2 Flutes [Flauti]
2 Oboes [Oboi]
2 Clarinets in A [Clarinetti]
2 Bassoons [Fagotti]

2 Horns in D [Corni]
2 Trumpets in D [Trombe]

Timpani

Violins I, II [Violino]
Violas
Cellos [Violoncello]
Basses [Basso]

OVERTURE TO

Idomeneo

Die Entführung aus dem Serail

The Abduction from the Seraglio

Comic singspiel in three acts

K384 (1781–2)

Libretto by Christoph Friedrich Bretzner
adapted by Johann Gottlieb Stephanie (the Younger)

First performance: Burgtheater, Vienna
16 July 1782

INSTRUMENTATION

Piccolo [Flauto piccolo]
2 Flutes [Flauti]
2 Oboes [Oboi]
2 Clarinets in C [Clarinetti]
2 Bassoons [Fagotti]

2 Horns in C [Corni]
2 Trumpets in C [Trombe]

Timpani

Percussion
    Triangle [Triangolo]
    Cymbals [Piatti]
    Large Drum [Tamburo grande]

Violins I, II [Violino]
Violas
Cellos [Violoncello]
Basses [Basso]

Die Entführung aus dem Serail

Overture to *Die Entführung aus dem Serail*

26   Overture to *Die Entführung aus dem Serail*

NOTE: For commentary on the concert ending of this overture, beginning with the sign ⊕ , see the footnote on Contents page iii.

Le Nozze di Figaro

Die Hochzeit des Figaro / The Marriage of Figaro

Opera buffa in four acts

K492 (1785–6)

Libretto by Lorenzo da Ponte
after the play *La Folle Journée ou Le Mariage de Figaro*
by Pierre de Beaumarchais (1784)

First performance: National Court Theater, Vienna
1 May 1786

Instrumentation

2 Flutes [Flauti]
2 Oboes [Oboi]
2 Clarinets in A [Clarinetti]
2 Bassoons [Fagotti]

2 Horns in D [Corni]
2 Trumpets in D [Trombe]

Timpani

Violins I, II [Violino]
Violas
Cellos [Violoncello]
Basses [Basso]

Le Nozze di Figaro

Don Giovanni

Il dissoluto punito, ossia Il Don Giovanni / Don Juan

Opera buffa in two acts

K527 (1787)

Libretto by Lorenzo da Ponte
based on earlier *Don Juan* librettos and other writings
related to plays by Tirso de Molina, Thomas Corneille and others

First performance: Count Nostitz National Theater, Prague
29 October 1787

INSTRUMENTATION

2 Flutes [Flauti]
2 Oboes [Oboi]
2 Clarinets in A [Clarinetti]
2 Bassoons [Fagotti]

2 Horns in D [Corni]
2 Trumpets in D [Trombe]

Timpani

Violins I, II [Violino]
Violas
Cellos and Basses
    [Violoncello e Basso, Vcl. e Bassi]

Don Giovanni

NOTE: For commentary on the concert ending of this overture, beginning with the sign ⊕, see the footnote on Contents page iii.

Così fan Tutte

. . . ossia La scuola degli amanti / Weibertreue

Opera buffa in two acts

K588 (1789–90)

Libretto by Lorenzo da Ponte

First performance: National Court Theater, Vienna
26 January 1790

INSTRUMENTATION

2 Flutes [Flauti]
2 Oboes [Oboi]
2 Clarinets in C [Clarinetti]
2 Bassoons [Fagotti]

2 Horns in G [Corni]
2 Trumpets in C [Trombe]

Timpani

Violins I, II [Violino]
Violas
Cellos and Basses [Violoncello e Basso]

Così fan Tutte

Die Zauberflöte

The Magic Flute

Singspiel in two acts

K620 (1791)

Libretto by Emanuel Schikaneder

First performance: Theater auf der Wieden, Vienna
30 September 1791

INSTRUMENTATION

2 Flutes [Flauti]
2 Oboes [Oboi]
2 Clarinets in B♭ ("B") [Clarinetti]
2 Bassoons [Fagotti]

2 Horns in E♭ ("Es") [Corni]
2 Trumpets in E♭ ("Es") [Trombe]

Timpani

3 Trombones
    [Trombone Alto/Tenore/Basso]

Violins I, II [Violino]
Violas
Cellos [Violoncello]
Basses [Basso]

Die Zauberflöte

La Clemenza di Tito

The Clemency of Titus

Opera seria in two acts

K621 (1791)

Libretto by Caterino Mazzola
based on the drama of the same name
by Pietro Metastasio (1734)

First performance: National Theater, Prague
6 September 1791

INSTRUMENTATION

2 Flutes [Flauti]
2 Oboes [Oboi]
2 Clarinets in B♭ ("B") [Clarinetti]
2 Bassoons [Fagotti]

2 Horns in C [Corni]
2 Trumpets in C [Trombe]

Timpani

Violins I, II [Violino]
Violas
Cellos [Violoncello]
Basses [Basso]

La Clemenza di Tito

END OF EDITION